CLIMATE Change
PROBLEMS and PROGRESS

Recycling Works!

Climate Change: Problems and Progress

The Danger of Greenhouse Gases

Extreme Weather

The Future of Biodiversity

The Organic Lifestyle

Preserving Energy

Recycling Works!

Renewable Energy in Action

Saving Water

The Vital Role of Deserts and Forests

What Is Climate Change?

WITHDRAWN

Recycling Works!

James Shoals

Mason Crest

Mason Crest
450 Parkway Drive, Suite D
Broomall, PA 19008
www.masoncrest.com

© 2020 by Mason Crest, an imprint of National Highlights, Inc.

All rights reserved. No part of this publication may be reproduced or transmitted in any form or by any means, electronic or mechanical, including photocopying, recording, taping, or any information storage and retrieval system, without permission from the publisher.

Printed and bound in the United States of America.

Series ISBN: 978-1-4222-4353-4
Hardback ISBN: 978-1-4222-4358-9
EBook ISBN: 978-1-4222-7453-8

First printing
1 3 5 7 9 8 6 4 2

Cover photographs by Dreamstime: Jordan Tan (left); Anasife (right). Shutterstock: ShutterPNPhotography (bottom); Hugette Roe (bkgd).

Library of Congress Cataloging-in-Publication Data is on file with the publisher.

QR Codes disclaimer:

You may gain access to certain third party content ("Third-Party Sites") by scanning and using the QR Codes that appear in this publication (the "QR Codes"). We do not operate or control in any respect any information, products, or services on such Third-Party Sites linked to by us via the QR Codes included in this publication, and we assume no responsibility for any materials you may access using the QR Codes. Your use of the QR Codes may be subject to terms, limitations, or restrictions set forth in the applicable terms of use or otherwise established by the owners of the Third-Party Sites. Our linking to such Third-Party Sites via the QR Codes does not imply an endorsement or sponsorship of such Third-Party Sites, or the information, products, or services offered on or through the Third-Party Sites, nor does it imply an endorsement or sponsorship of this publication by the owners of such Third-Party Sites.

CONTENTS

Words to Understand 6
Introduction 8
Product Generation
and Waste 10
Landfills 12
Combustion of Solid Waste 14
Biodegradable Waste 16
Reduce 18
Reuse 20
Recycle 22
Recycling Paper 24
Glass Recycling 26
Steel Recycling 28
Aluminum Recycling 30
E-waste 32
Construction and Demolition
Waste 34
Reuse and Recycle Clothes 36
Plastic Recycling 38
Waste Reduction 40
Animal Waste 42

Text-Dependent Questions 44
Research Projects 45
Find Out More 46
Series Glossary of Key Terms 47
Index 48

KEY ICONS TO LOOK FOR

Words to Understand: These words with their easy-to-understand definitions will increase the reader's understanding of the text, while building vocabulary skills.

Sidebars: This boxed material within the main text allows readers to build knowledge, gain insights, explore possibilities, and broaden their perspectives by weaving together additional information to provide realistic and holistic perspectives.

Educational Videos: Readers can view videos by scanning our QR codes, providing them with additional educational content to supplement the text. Examples include news coverage, moments in history, speeches, iconic moments, and much more!

Text-Dependent Questions: These questions send the reader back to the text for more careful attention to the evidence presented here.

Research Projects: Readers are pointed toward areas of further inquiry connected to each chapter. Suggestions are provided for projects that encourage deeper research and analysis.

Series Glossary of Key Terms: This back-of-the-book glossary contains terminology used throughout this series. Words found here increase the reader's ability to read and comprehend higher-level books and articles in this field.

WORDS TO UNDERSTAND

asbestos a mineral that does not burn easily and can be used for making fabrics and other materials

asphalt a black sticky substance used for making roads

bauxite an ore from which the metal aluminum is obtained

biodegradable the substance that can be broken down by bacteria so that it is not harmful to the environment

cadmium a metallic element that is used in batteries

carbon footprint the amount of CO_2 that a person, organization, building, etc., produces

combustion the process of burning

compost a mixture of decaying plants and animals used as a fertilizer

compress to press or squeeze something

contaminant a substance that makes something dirty, polluted, or poisonous

countertop a flat working surface in kitchens or bathrooms

deplete to reduce the amount of something

disposable something that is designed to be thrown away after it has been used once or a few times

economic related to business, industry, and trade

feces the solid waste released from the body of humans and animals

flannel a soft cotton fabric used for making clothes

habitat the natural home of an animal, plant or other organism

incineration to burn something completely

landfill a large hole in the ground where waste is buried

organic related to or derived from living matter

ream a large amount of something

retail related to sale of goods directly to the public for its own use

scrap a small amount of food that is left after the meal

sewage the wastewater and excrements removed from a house or building through a system of underground pipes called sewers

toxic poisonous and harmful to people, animals, and environment

upholstery the cloth that is used for covering chairs and sofas

INTRODUCTION

Global warming poses a great threat to our environment and to our existence. Various human activities have resulted in major climate changes. It has led to a rise in global temperatures, melting of polar ice sheets and ice caps, a rise in sea levels, and abnormal evaporation and precipitation.

One of the major threats to global climate comes from the massive waste generation by humans. The large amount of waste generated by us directly contributes to the emission of greenhouse gases (GHGs) and wastage of resources.

Reducing and recycling solid waste is an active way to reduce GHG emissions. It saves waste from ending up in landfills where it produces GHGs. The manufacture, distribution, and use of products as well as management of the resulting waste lead to GHG emissions.

Impact of Waste

Any unwanted or useless material that we want to throw away is waste. The large amounts of trash or garbage that we discard contributes directly and indirectly to global warming. Our waste generation is closely linked to the emission of GHGs.

GHGs

Carbon dioxide (CO_2) and methane are two powerful GHGs produced during waste generation. CO_2 is the most abundant GHG in the atmosphere and is produced directly when fuels are burnt to generate energy. Methane is produced during the decomposition of organic waste, such as wood, paper, and food waste.

Climate Change

An increased concentration of CO_2 and methane in the atmosphere leads to global climate change. These GHGs trap the sun's heat in the atmosphere. This heat leads to a rise in global temperatures. Global warming is causing polar ice sheets to melt. Low-lying regions of the world are under threat of being submerged due to rising sea levels.

Zero Waste

If all of us generate less waste and thus reduce our **carbon footprint**, the threat of global warming can be overcome to a certain extent. The way we produce, consume, and dispose of our goods accounts for a huge amount of GHG emissions. Therefore, we should switch to environment-friendly practices.

Climate Facts

- It is estimated that food wasted by the United States and Europe could feed the world three times over.

- The United States is the world's largest trash-producing country at 1,609 pounds (727 kg) of trash per person each year.

Recycling Works!

Product Generation and Waste

Large amounts of goods are produced every day. Manufacturing a product requires a lot of resources and energy. Every time we throw away a product, we waste the energy and resources that went into the manufacturing of that product. Each process in product manufacturing consumes energy and material inputs, and generates a lot of waste.

Raw Material

Man has been destroying natural environments and cutting down trees to extract raw materials needed for the production of goods. This has automatically led to global warming. Mining for metals produces toxic gases such as sulfur dioxide. The extraction of coal and oil also releases many toxic gases.

Use of Energy

Every stage in a product's life cycle, from obtaining the raw materials to manufacturing, requires energy. All these processes require fuels such as coal, petroleum, and diesel. The **combustion** of fuels and other chemical processes releases various GHGs into the atmosphere.

Distribution

Fuel-powered trucks and vehicles are used for the distribution of raw materials and finished products. This leads to the emission of GHGs, such as CO (carbon monoxide) and CO_2. The packaging of products for distribution also generates large amounts of waste.

Climate Facts

- Due to the renewable nature of food waste, it generates lower emissions upon incineration as compared to other wastes.

- The methane released from coal mines accounts for 8 percent of global methane emissions.

Recycling Works!   11

Landfills

The majority of waste generated by us ends up in landfills—large pits in the ground for dumping waste. They are carefully constructed and waste is separated and **compressed** to avoid any interaction with groundwater and the atmosphere. However, as the waste stored in landfills decomposes, it releases many harmful gases.

Landfill Gas

Methane makes up about 40–60 percent of landfill gas and 35 percent of it is CO_2. Methane is a highly flammable gas and leads to global warming. Landfill gas also contains traces of water vapor, oxygen, nitrogen, sulfur, and other **contaminants**.

Harmful Effects

The toxic water that seeps through landfills often leaks and contaminates groundwater resources. In 2005, the gases emitted in wastewater treatment and through landfills accounted for 2.3 percent of the GHG emissions in the US.

Harnessing Landfill Gas

Initiatives are being taken for reducing the environmental impact of the GHG. Since methane is a very potent GHG, it is reduced to CO_2 to ease its overall effect on global warming. This process is known as flaring. The methane emitted from landfills is also being recovered for heating and generating electricity. Various gas-to-energy projects aim at utilizing landfill gas to generate electricity.

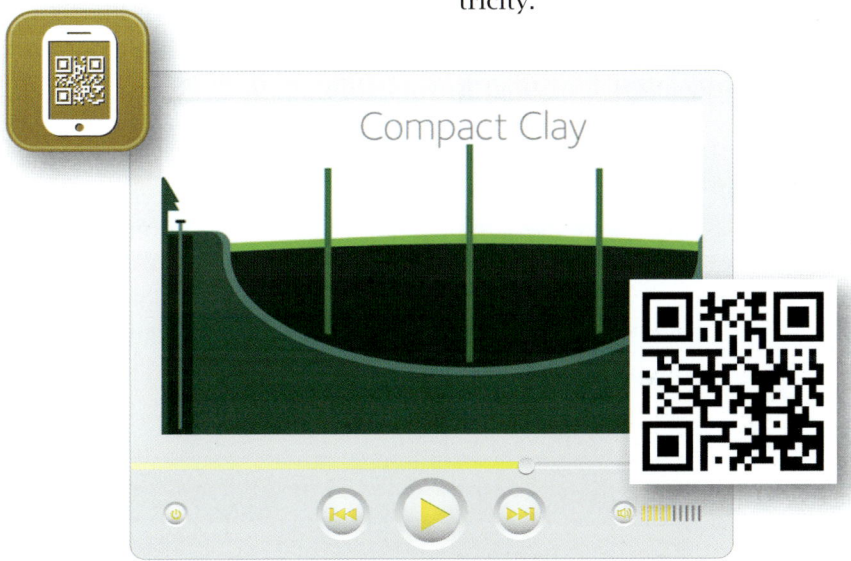

Landfill processes

Climate Facts

- In 1986, the concentration and spread of landfill gas destroyed property in Loscoe, England.

- Methane traps thirty times more heat than CO_2 and contributes to 18 percent more energy.

Recycling Works!

Combustion of Solid Waste

The large amounts of waste that we produce is often disposed of by burning it in large furnaces known as incinerators. Most of the solid waste on Earth is removed by combustion. However, unsafe combustion practices harm the atmosphere.

CO_2

Burning organic matter, such as coal, oil, and wood converts solid carbon into CO_2. A ton of organic waste produces the same amount of CO_2 upon burning. Thus, the **incineration** of solid wastes produces more CO_2 than produced by landfills.

Nitrous Oxide

The combustion of solid waste, **sewage** treatment, and agricultural processes produces another GHG known as nitrous oxide. Nitrous oxide (N_2O) is a major air pollutant. It has also led to the large-scale depletion of the ozone layer. This depletion allows harmful ultraviolet rays from the sun to reach the earth.

Combustion of Solid Waste

Many people burn a collection of solid wastes, without knowing about its harmful effects. Uncontrolled burning of waste releases harmful gases such as CO_2 and CO. Chemicals, hydrocarbons, and sulfur products in the discarded waste materials also release many toxic gases, which are harmful to the environment and to public health.

Climate Facts

- In 1997, the United States emitted about one-fifth of the total global GHGs.

- Nitrous oxide is also known as "laughing gas"—it creates euphoric effects upon inhalation.

Recycling Works!

Biodegradable Waste

Biodegradable waste can easily break down and decompose in natural conditions. It is also known as **organic** waste since it comes from living organisms. Food waste, paper waste, plant and crop waste, manure, sewage, wood, and timber are all biodegradable wastes. If this waste finds its way in landfills, it releases large quantities of methane.

Composting Process

Compost is prepared when different kinds of organic wastes are mixed together and allowed to decompose in the presence of oxygen. These waste materials are broken down by worms, insects, bacteria, and fungi. As these organisms feed on the mixture of organic waste, it begins to rot and gradually turns into sweet-smelling humus. This mixture includes elements like air, water, carbon, and nitrogen.

Composting and Greenhouse Effect

Composting also reduces GHG emissions. Many people believe that throwing food scraps and paper products into a **landfill** is harmless because the materials are biodegradable. However, when these materials break down in a landfill, they rot without oxygen and release methane, which is more powerful than CO_2.

Biogas

The breakdown of organic material in the absence of oxygen through the action of microorganisms is known as anaerobic digestion. This process is used to generate a gaseous fuel known as biogas. Biogas is mainly made up of methane and CO_2. It is an effective way of converting waste into energy, and it reduces the impact of waste on global warming.

Benefits of Composting

Composting is a useful way to prevent biodegradable waste from ending up in landfills. It is nature's way of recycling organic waste. It creates humus that is rich in nutrients and can be used as a natural fertilizer in gardens and parks. This reduces the use of chemical fertilizers and helps in conserving natural resources.

Climate Facts

- The first anaerobic digester was made by a leper colony in Bombay, India, in 1959.
- Every pound (0.4 kg) of solid waste that goes into a landfill results in two pounds (0.8 kg) of GHGs.

Recycling Works!

Reduce

There is a need to follow the three Rs of waste management—reduce, reuse, and recycle—to prevent global warming. The first and foremost step that we must take to prevent unnecessary waste is to reduce consumption. An easy way to do it is by cutting down on the amount of garbage that we make. Less waste means less cleaning up.

Buy Less

In order to reduce waste, we must first limit our buying to only necessary, long-lasting, and reusable items. We should try to use all the things we buy. Avoid buying more food than is possible to eat.

Avoid Disposable Products

We must try to use reusable items whenever possible. **Disposable** plates and spoons stay in landfills for a very long time. By using reusable bags for shopping, we can save large amounts of plastic waste from clogging our bodies of water.

Packaging

The things that we buy generally come in elaborate plastic or other packing. This packaging usually ends up in dustbins. To avoid such waste, we must buy things with reusable or recyclable packaging. We must buy large packs or quantities of products like shampoos and detergents.

CLIMATE CHANGE: Problems and Progress

Save Resources

We must also try to save resources by simple practices such as switching off the lights when not in use. Avoid wastage of natural resources by turning off taps and switching off electronics when not in use. Although these things do not directly contribute to the production of waste, they help in saving energy resources and preventing air pollution.

Tips on reducing waste

Climate Facts

- You should use both sides of paper when printing.

- Carpooling is an effective way of saving oil and energy.

Recycling Works! 19

Reuse

Reusing things is an effective way of preventing waste. "Reuse" means to find a new way of using waste items, so that we do not have to throw them away. We can save large amounts of landfill space if we find alternative uses of waste.

Donate

Clothes that do not fit us any more or items that we do not need can be donated to the other sections of society. Backyard sales and charities are other means of giving away those items that are of little use to us, such as old furniture, electronic appliances, and other items.

Repair

Broken toys, torn clothes, worn-out shoes, and electronic appliances are some of the things that can be repaired or mended for further use. Before throwing away things, we must explore all possibilities of reusing them. Repairing can save many things from going into dustbins.

Alternative Uses

Waste items can be reused in a variety of ways. Old and torn clothes can be used as cleaning rags, while plastic bags can be used as garbage bins. Newspapers can be used for packaging. Empty containers can be used for refilling. Wastewater can be used in industries, for watering parks, or for car washes.

Climate Facts

- The exchange of things such as books and clothes not only saves money and resources, but also prevents waste.

- Nokia launched a campaign for collecting waste materials for recycling. It accepted old cell phones while selling new ones.

Recycling Works!

Recycle

Recycling is the process through which waste is used again. It is a way of transforming waste products into new products. It is beneficial as it not only reduces the amount of garbage going into landfills and incinerators, but also reduces the extraction of raw materials from the earth.

What Can Be Recycled?

The most well-known recycled materials are glass, paper, plastic, and aluminum. Batteries, biodegradable waste, concrete, electronics, and steel can also be recycled.

Separation at Source

Collection of different materials for recycling is a difficult process. It is always beneficial to separate recyclable material right from the beginning. In addition, biodegradable materials must be separated from nonbiodegradable items. Hazardous waste must not be thrown away along with normal waste.

Recycling Loop

The three arrows in a recycling logo stand for the three processes of recycling—collection, recycling, and resale. The recycling loop starts when we throw waste in our garbage bins. It is collected by waste collectors and sent to processing facilities, where it is recycled into new products. The recycling loop closes when consumers buy the recycled products again. A recycling symbol on a product means that the product either is made from recycled material or is recyclable.

Climate Facts

- Around 60 percent of the garbage in landfills can be composted or recycled.

- We should wash and reuse plastic cups, utensils, and bags to reduce waste.

Recycling Works! 23

Recycling Paper

We use large amounts of paper every day for writing, drawing, printing, and packaging. Paper that we throw away everyday contributes to global warming in a big way. It is made up from a plant material known as cellulose. According to the United States Environmental Protection Agency (EPA), approximately 33 percent of household waste consists of paper and paperboard.

Conserving Forests

Paper recycling saves trees and the fuels required in the production of paper. Recycling one ton of paper saves seventeen trees and three thousand gallons of water. Recycling paper will ensure that there are more trees left in the environment to absorb CO_2 and release oxygen into the atmosphere. Cutting down trees to make paper also leads to the destruction of the natural **habitats** of many animals.

Recycled Paper Products

Recycled paper can be used to make a variety of products such as copier paper, paper towels and napkins, toilet paper, and others. The recycling sign found on cereal boxes, cardboard containers, and notebook paper indicates that the paper has been made from recycled fiber.

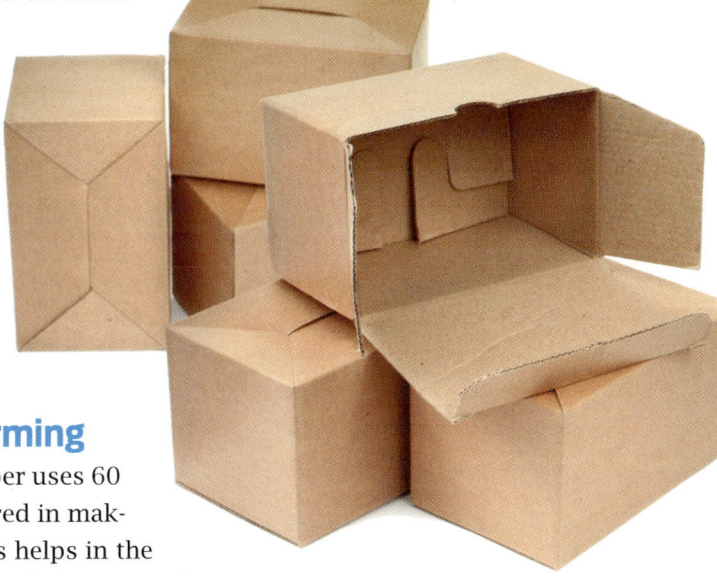

Preventing Global Warming

The production of recycled paper uses 60 percent less energy than required in making paper from fresh pulp. This helps in the conservation of fossil fuels. Recycled paper reduces water pollution by 35 percent, air pollution by 74 percent and prevents many toxic pollutants from contaminating the environment. Paper that finds its way in landfills, results in the production of methane gas.

Climate Facts

- Wood fiber can be recycled only up to five times, after which it becomes too weak to be recycled again.

- Using one ream of 100 percent post-consumer recycled paper for your printer or copy machine keeps 4.8 pounds (2.2 kg) of CO_2 out of our atmosphere.

Glass Recycling

Glass waste such as broken glass, bottles, and other equipment poses a great risk of injury to waste handlers and rag pickers. Glass waste can stay intact in landfills for more than four thousand years. Glass can be recycled a number of times without affecting its quality or purity.

Recycling Benefits

Recycling a glass bottle can save enough energy to run a computer for half an hour. It also causes 20 percent less air pollution and 50 percent less water pollution. Producing one ton of glass from waste not only saves 383 pounds (174) kg of mining waste, but also creates 694 pounds (315 kg) less of CO_2.

Collection of Used Glass

To avoid glass from entering the garbage, various collection schemes and glass disposal programs have been arranged. In many countries, the refund offered upon returning used glass bottles for recycling has helped encourage their recycling.

Glass Recycle Process

The waste glass is first cleaned of all impurities and then melted to form cullets. These cullets are sold off to glass bottle manufacturers who use them along with soda ash and limestone as raw materials to manufacture new glass containers. Glass can be recycled into new bottles in just thirty days. Recycled glass is also used to make fiberglass insulation, **countertops**, tiles, and ingredients for road construction.

Climate Facts

- Glass waste of different colors is separated by their colors since glass retains its color after recycling.

- Pyrex, mirrors, and crystal cannot be recycled.

Recycling Works!

Steel Recycling

Steel is an extremely prized alloy due to its strength, quality, and durability. It is one of the most commonly used materials in the world. Steel is largely used in the construction of roads, buildings, and other infrastructure. It also forms a major component of vehicles, surgical equipment, and household appliances.

Usage

Steel is used in many building projects due to its strength. Steel containers can hold a variety of products, from food to paint to shoe polish. They simply need to be rinsed before they are ready to be recycled.

Benefits of Recycling Steel

The steel industry's major raw material is **scrap** metal, which is collected through recycling steel. Steel recycling needs 75 percent less energy than making steel from iron ore. This energy is enough to power eighteen million homes. One ton of recycled steel saves 2,497 pounds (1,133 kg) of iron ore, 1,400 pounds (635 kg) of coal and 119 pounds (54 kg) of limestone. Recycling steel prevents the need to mine additional iron and coal that are needed to make new steel.

CLIMATE CHANGE: Problems and Progress

Steel Recycling

Steel recycling saves landfill space as well as provides a scrap resource to the steel industry. Steel is a key component of car parts and household appliances, and recycled steel has the same strength as new steel when used in these devices. Steel does not need to be separated by color or size before it is recycled; all of it can be melted down at once.

Climate Facts

- Americans use one hundred million steel cans every day.

- The amount of wood and paper we throw away each year is enough to heat fifty million homes for twenty years.

Recycling Works!   29

Aluminum Recycling

Aluminum is a lightweight metal used largely in the production of beverage cans since it is durable and flexible. Aluminum cans are the most recycled consumer product in the United States. Other aluminum products such as siding, foil, car components, and lawn furniture can also be recycled. Aluminum is 100 percent recyclable and can be recycled repeatedly.

Benefits

An aluminum can that finds its way in a landfill will stay there for almost five hundred years before breaking down. Recycling aluminum generates enough energy to power a TV for three hours. If an aluminum can is burnt down, it releases many **toxic** gases. Recycling forty-five aluminum cans can save up to 1 gallon (3.78 l) of the crude oil that goes into its production. It takes 95 percent less energy to produce recycled aluminum than to derive aluminum from **bauxite** ore. This also results in reduced carbon emissions.

Recycling Process

We use over eighty billion aluminum soda cans every year. Discarded aluminum cans are cleaned and melted at high temperatures. They are then turned into thick metal blocks known as ingots. These metal blocks are sent to can sheet manufacturers who make cans from these blocks and sell them to beverage industries. Aluminum cans are processed, recycled, and find their way back to stores in less than sixty days.

Climate Facts

- Americans recycle more than $6.3 billion worth of aluminum each year.

- Americans throw away about forty million beverage cans, which, if placed end to end, would reach the Moon and back nearly twenty times.

Recycling Works!

E-waste

E-waste consists of all the electronic devices and appliances, such as old computers, kitchen appliances, cell phones, and TVs, that are no longer useful. Rapid technological development has made electronics the largest-growing waste stream. Electronic devices have very short lives and are soon replaced by thinner, sleeker, and faster devices.

Threat to Environment

Illegal and improper disposal of e-waste is a great threat to our environment. Electronic devices contain toxic chemicals such as lead, mercury, and **cadmium**, which contaminate the environment. A large amount of e-waste finds its way to landfills, incinerators, or is illegally exported to developing countries for recycling. Burning electronic waste to recover precious metals also releases toxic gases. According to an IT (information technology) research company, the manufacturing, distribution, and use of information technology accounts for 2 percent of global warming.

Recycling E-waste

Only about 15 percent of the total e-waste generated in a year is recycled. Proper recycling of one million desktop computers can reduce GHG emissions equal to the annual emissions of over seventeen thousand cars. Often, only some parts of the electronic appliances are recycled while the rest are dumped. Proper care is required while recycling and extracting the different components of electronic devices, such as glass, copper, aluminum, and plastic.

Corporate Programs

To avoid the growing problem of e-waste disposal, many companies such as Apple, Dell, Whirlpool, and Sony have introduced recycling programs. Sony has established "drop-off centers" at its various retail stores, where it takes back its branded products and recycles them. Nokia, the communications and information technology giant, has also introduced a similar scheme wherein customers are encouraged to return their old handsets.

Climate Facts

- Our e-waste also exists outside the Earth in the form of nonworking satellites that float in space. Plans are being made to recycle these satellites.

- According to the United Nations Environmental Program, around twenty to fifty million tons of e-waste are disposed of every year.

Construction and Demolition Waste

Construction and demolition generate large quantities of waste often called C&D waste, which is a mixture of clay, concrete, timber, stone, tiles, cement, steel, glass, shingles, and other such material. Construction waste may also include toxic substances such as **asbestos** and lead.

Contribution to Global Warming

C&D waste directly contributes to global warming by releasing GHGs into the atmosphere. The waste generated contains large amounts of timber, cardboard, metal, and concrete. Wood and other construction waste account for a large portion of the methane gas that leaks from landfills. Building activities also generate hazardous wastes such as asbestos.

Recycling C&D Waste

C&D waste recycling reduces the burden of bulky waste on landfills as well as saves the energy resources required in the production of new materials. Concrete and **asphalt** can be recycled and used in road construction. Soil and dirt created during construction is often used as landfill covers. Wood and timber recovered from demolition sites can be reused or treated as organic waste. Plastics, glass, and metals can be sent to their respective recycling plants.

Recycling construction waste

 Climate Facts

- In India, less than 50 percent of the C&D waste is recycled.

- Recycling C&D material from one home will save methane emissions equal to taking one car off the road for a year.

Recycling Works! 35

Reuse and Recycle Clothes

Textile waste includes all the things made of fabric such as clothes, beddings, shoes, soft toys, etc. They include a variety of fibers such as cotton, nylon, wool, linen, and **flannel**. More than one million tons of textile waste each year comes from household sources. Garment manufacturers and **retail** industries also produce textile waste.

Recycling Benefits

Textiles create grave dumping problems. Synthetic fibers do not decompose easily and stay in landfills for thousands of years, whereas natural fabrics such as wool and cotton decompose readily and produce methane gas. The recycling of textiles helps to prevent pollution. The use of recycled material saves energy resources and imported raw materials.

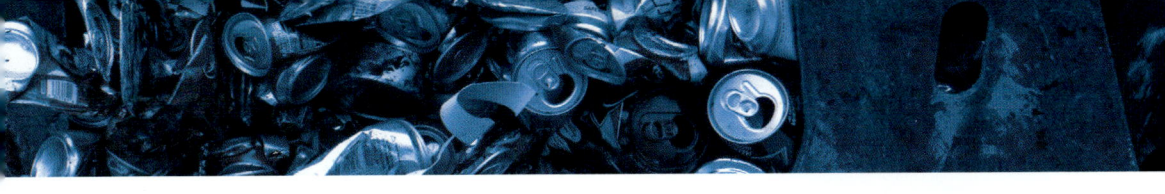

Reuse

Textile wastes can be reused in a variety of ways. They can be repaired and reused as rags by paint stores, machine shops, and industries. They can also be donated to the needy. They can be sold off at jumbo sales or on websites. This can greatly reduce the burden on our landfills. Textile wastes can also be used for making **upholstery** for new homes.

Recycle

According to the EPA, almost 97 percent of textiles made of both natural and man-made fibers can be recycled. Textile recycling requires the least amount of energy resources and does not create harmful or hazardous byproducts. The different materials are separated based on their quality, type, and condition. Wearable clothes and shoes are often sold to Third World countries. Unwearable textiles are shredded and used in car insulation, furniture fillings, panel linings, etc. Buttons and zippers are often stripped off for further use.

Climate Facts

- The average life of a garment is about three years.

- Clothes and fabrics must be kept separately from normal garbage to avoid staining and contact with moisture.

Recycling Works! 37

Plastic Recycling

Plastic is a light, durable, moldable, and **economic** substance. Wide varieties of plastics are used to produce a number of products such as food containers, pipes, shopping bags, bottle crates, sacks, water pipes, windscreen wipers, and others.

Plastic: Threat to Environment

Natural resources such as crude oil, natural gas, and oil are used to make plastics. Once **depleted**, these natural resources cannot be replaced. Most plastics are nonbiodegradable and stay in the environment for thousands of years. The production as well as disposal of plastics produce large amounts of GHGs.

Labelled Plastics

Not all plastic materials can be recycled. Plastic products are labelled with a number that helps in identifying the materials they are made of and determine whether they are toxic or not. Normally, plastic containers labeled as 1, 2, and 3 are recyclable, whereas those labeled 4, 5, 6, and 7 are not easily recycled. Plastic products such as egg trays, cups, and plates are difficult to recycle.

Plastic Recycling Process

Used plastic bottles and containers are collected and sent to a facility where they are washed and checked. Then they are cut into small pieces that are melted in a large furnace and turned into long strands. The strands are cut into pellets, which are sent to factories to make new items. Recycled plastic can be used to make tables, chairs, stationary, and packing material.

Plastic recycling process

Climate Facts

- The carbon footprint of plastic accounts for 13 pounds (6 kg) of CO_2 per 2.2 pounds (1 kg) of plastic.
- About 6 percent of the world's oil is used for the production of plastic.

Recycling Works!   39

Waste Reduction

To reduce the contribution of each person in global warming, various methods and policies are adopted in different countries. Awareness regarding waste and its contribution to global warming has made businesses and individuals more responsible throughout the world.

Plastic Bags

Plastic bags are produced all around the world. The mix of materials in a plastic bag prevents it from decomposing for thousands of years. These bags not only clog our streets and waterways, and endanger the local wildlife, but also contribute to climate change. Several countries and regions have banned single-use plastic shopping bags. Customers are asked to pay for the plastic bags that they use.

"Pay as You Throw" Programs

Some communities charge their residents for the waste they generate. Under such schemes, the residents have to pay some fee for the disposal of the local solid waste that they throw away. Waste is measured in terms of size and weight. It gives the users an incentive to reduce waste and recycle more.

Waste Collection

The separation of waste at the time of disposal helps to prevent nonbiodegradable and other hazardous waste from ending in landfills. Different-colored bins are placed in public places and consumers are educated about the proper disposal of food waste, nonbiodegradable, and hazardous waste. Nearly two-thirds of all household wastes can be recycled and are often collected separately by different workers.

Climate Facts

- Plastic bags contributed to the flooding of Dhaka, Bangladesh in 1988 and 1998.

- The producers of products are also responsible for the disposal of their products.

Recycling Works! 41

Animal Waste

Animal farming and cattle rearing increase global climate change. The production of meat, eggs, and milk requires not only the direct rearing and slaughtering of animals, but also grain production for animal feed. The waste produced by these animals, its disposal, and storage contribute to global warming.

Animal Waste and GHGs

The animal agriculture sector is responsible for 35–40 percent of the annual methane emissions. Ruminants such as sheep, goats, and cows produce methane in their stomachs as part of their digestive processes. Typically, cattle reared for dairy products are fed a high-protein diet consisting of corn and soybeans resulting in an increase in GHGs. Untreated animal **feces** also flow into the nearby water bodies, causing water pollution.

Animal Rearing

Approximately 56 billion land animals are reared and slaughtered for human consumption annually. Farm animals and animal production facilities cover one-third of the planet's land surface. This has led to deforestation, land degradation, and an increase in CO_2 emissions. Overgrazing by farm animals has also led to the depletion of wooded areas.

Waste-to-Energy

Animal feces and manure release large amounts of GHGs. Ways are being devised to recycle animal waste into fuel. Methane generated from animal manure has the power to heat homes, cook meals, and generate electricity. The animal waste that is left to rot produces methane and N_2O by the action of bacteria. The manure that is stacked and stored in dry form is often used in agricultural soil. It does not produce significant amounts of methane.

Climate Facts

- One dairy cow produces approximately 119 pounds (54 kg) of wet manure per day.

- The animal agriculture sector accounts for about 9 percent of the total CO_2 emissions.

TEXT-DEPENDENT QUESTIONS

1. What is a landfill?

2. What is compost?

3. What are the three Rs of waste management?

4. What do the three arrows in the recycling logo stand for?

5. About how many cans do American use every year, according to the text?

6. What are some of the materials contained in construction waste?

7. What numbers on plastic material show that they are recyclable?

8. What kinds of animals are responsible for adding methane to the atmosphere?

RESEARCH PROJECTS

1. Pick one area of recycling described in the text. Then look further into it, focusing on the United States statistics in that area. Is recycling in that manner going up or going down? Make a chart about three programs that you find, either national or regional, that are trying to improve this particular area.

2. Research your area's local recycling program. What materials do they recycle? How are they collected? Beyond any weekly pickup, what materials are recycled at special sites (for example, paint or batteries)? Make a chart of them all and check off those things that your family recycles. Can you recycle more?

3. Help spread the word! Research the facts about your local recycling and make a poster that encourages and instructs people how they can help . . . and how they can do more! Use colorful graphics and attention-grabbing stats to make your case.

FIND OUT MORE

Books

Byers, Ann. *Reuse It: The History of Modern Recycling.* New York: Cavendish Square, 2018.

Kellogg, Kathryn. *101 Ways to Go Zero Waste.* New York: Countryman Press, 2019.

Latham, Donna. *Garbage: Follow the Path of Your Trash With Environmental Activities.* White River Junction, VT: Nomad Press, 2019.

On the Internet

Global Recycling Day (March 18)
www.globalrecyclingday.com/

Environmental Protection Agency
www.epa.gov/recycle

Earth 911
earth911.com/

SERIES GLOSSARY OF KEY TERMS

bioaccumulation the process of the buildup of toxic chemical substances in the body

biodiversity the diversity of plant and animal life in a habitat (or in the world as a whole)

ecosystem refers to a community of organisms, their interaction with each other, and their physical environment

famine a severe shortage of food (as through crop failure), resulting in hunger, starvation, and death

hydrophobic tending to repel, and not absorb water or become wet by water

irrigation the method of providing water to agricultural fields

La Niña periodic, significant cooling of the surface waters of the equatorial Pacific Ocean, which causes abnormal weather patterns

migration the movement of persons or animals from one country or locality to another

pollutants the foreign materials which are harmful to the environment

precipitation the falling to earth of any form of water (rain, snow, hail, sleet, or mist)

stressors processes or events that cause stress

susceptible yielding readily to or capable of

symbiotic the interaction between organisms (especially of different species) that live together and happen to benefit from each other

vulnerable someone or something that can be easily harmed or attacked

INDEX

animal waste, 42-43
biodegradable waste, 16
biogas, 17
C&D waste, 34-35
carbon dioxide, 8-9, 11, 13-15, 17, 24, 43
carbon footprint, 9
combustion, 14-15
composting, 16-17
contaminants, 12
disposable products, 18
donating, 20
e-waste, 32-33
food waste, 8, 41
forest conservation, 24
fuels, 11
glass waste, 27
greenhouse effect, 16
greenhouse gases, 8-9, 11, 13-14, 33, 42-43
labelled plastics, 38
landfills, 12-13, 16, 20, 22, 29
methane, 8, 12-13, 17, 42
nitrous oxide, 14
organic waste, 16
packaging, 18
paper, 24-25
plastic bags, 40

plastics, 38-39
programs, 33, 40
raw materials, 10
recycling, 22
  aluminum, 30-31
  benefits of, 26
  C&D waste, 35
  clothes, 36-37
  e-waste, 33
  glass, 26-27
  paper, 24-25
  plastics, 39
  steel, 28-29
  symbol of, 23
repairing, 20
reusing, 20-21
saving resources, 19
separating materials, 23
sewage, 14
solid waste, 14-15
textiles, 36-37
toxic gases, 10, 13, 30, 32
vehicles, 11, 29-30
waste collection, 41
waste impact, 8
waste management, 18, 20-25
waste reduction, 40-41

Photo Credits

Photographs sourced by Macaw Media, except for:
Dreamstime.com: Michelle Arconti 37B, Nehru 43B.